SWISS FAMILY ROBINSON

JOHANN RUDOLF WYSS

Adapted by Dr. Marion Kimberly

GALLERY BOOKS
An Imprint of W. H. Smith Publishers Inc.
112 Madison Avenue
New York City 10016

© 1990 Ediciones B, S.A., Barcelona, Spain

This edition published 1991 by Gallery Books,
an imprint of W.H.Smith Publishers, Inc.,
112 Madison Avenue, New York, New York 10016

ISBN 0-8317-1458-1

Gallery Books are available for bulk purchase for sales
promotions and premium use. For details write or telephone
the Manager of Special Sales, W.H.Smith Publishers, Inc.,
112 Madison Avenue, New York, New York 10016. (212) 532-6600

Produced by Hawk Books Limited, London

Printed in Spain

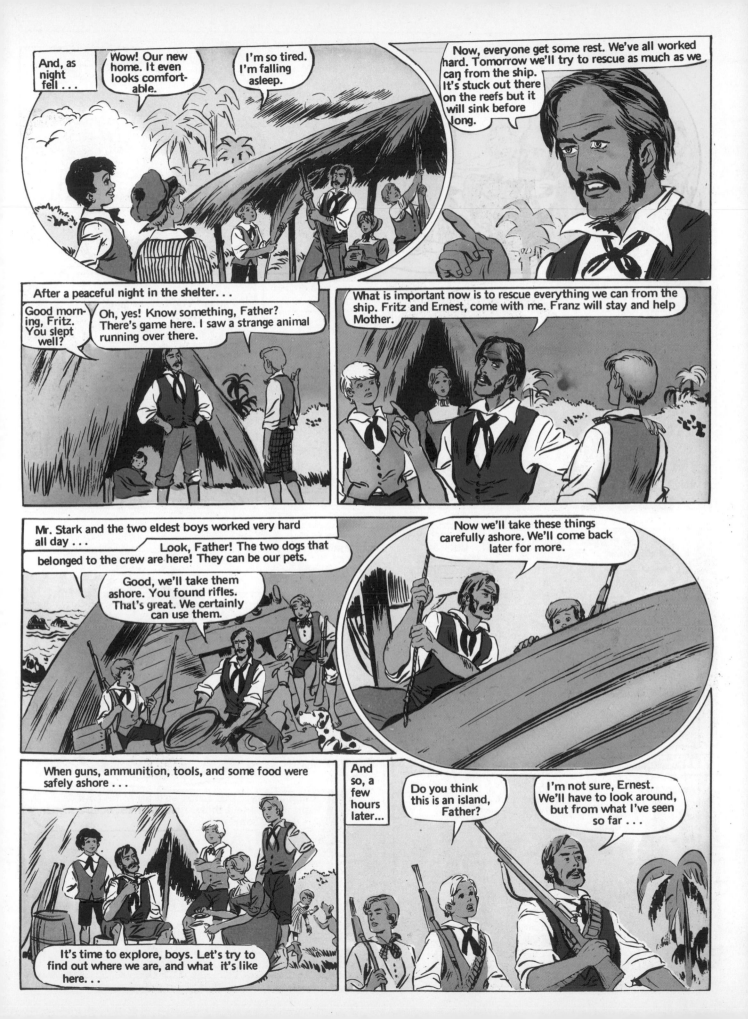

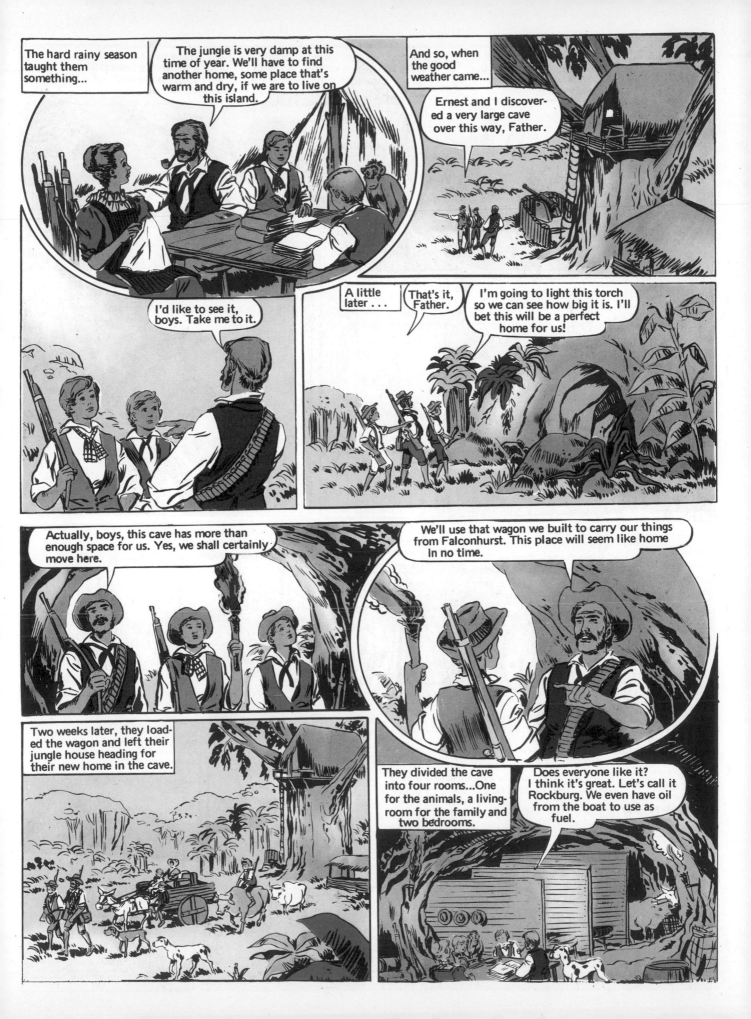

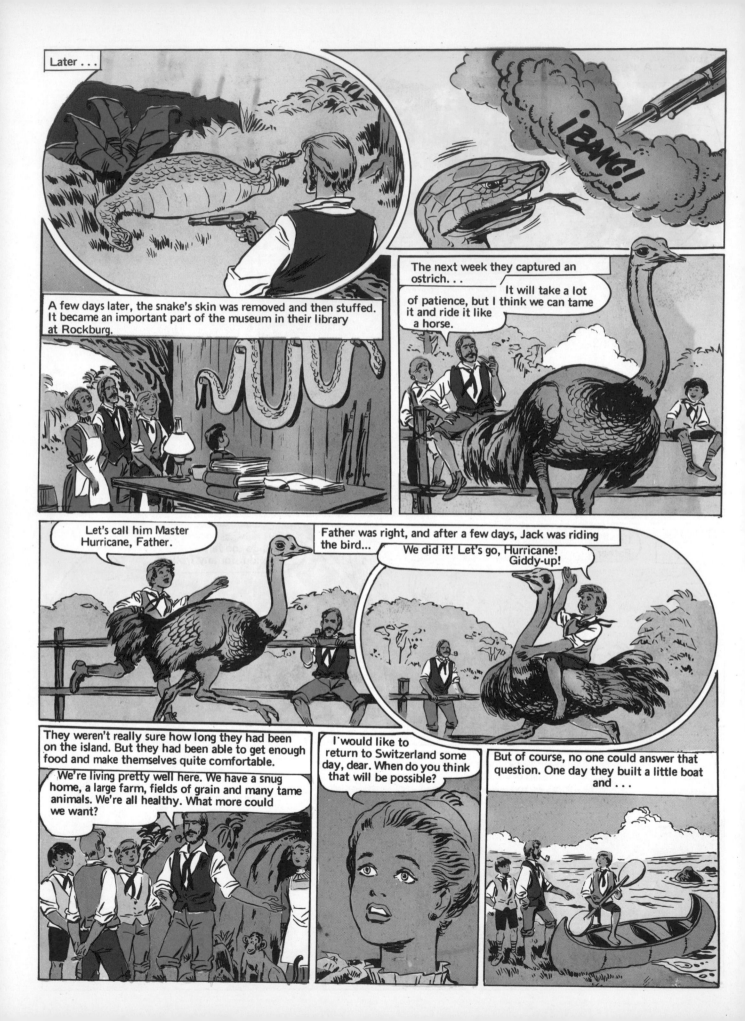

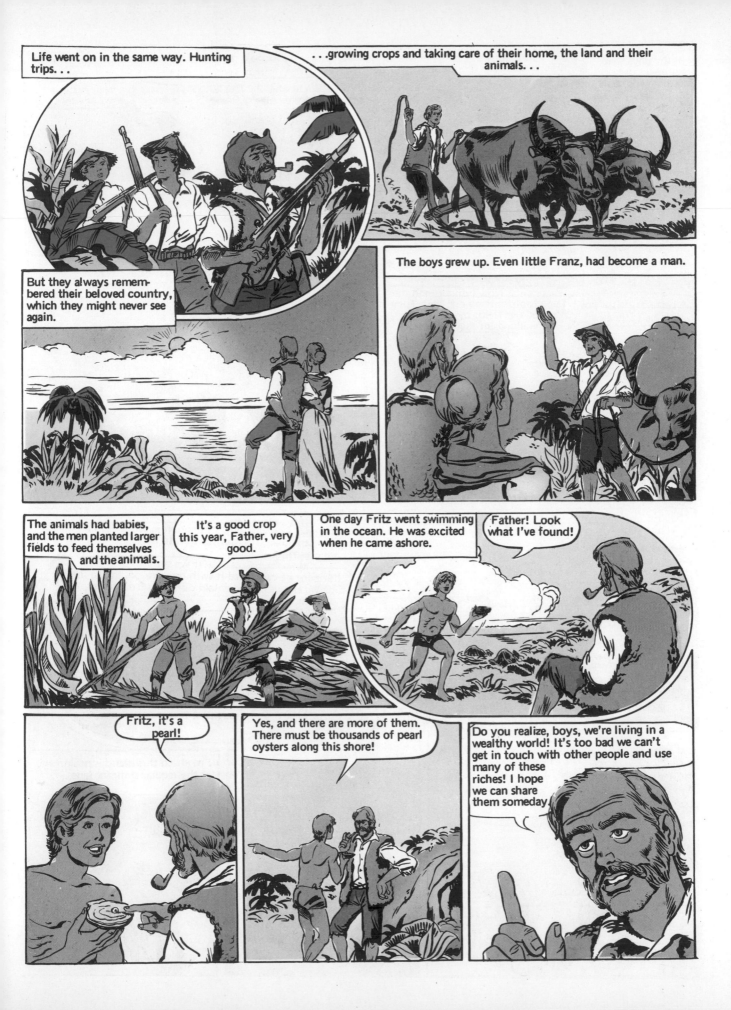